EXPLORING OUR RAINFOREST

HORNBILL

SUSAN H. GRAY

Published in the United States of America by Cherry Lake Publishing
Ann Arbor, Michigan
www.cherrylakepublishing.com

Content Adviser: Dr. Stephen S. Ditchkoff, Professor of Wildlife Ecology, Auburn University, Alabama
Reading Adviser: Marla Conn, ReadAbility, Inc.

Photo Credits: ©apiguide/Shutterstock Images, cover, 1, 26; ©iliuta goean/Shutterstock Images, 5; ©BirdLife International and NatureServe (2014) Bird Species Distribution Maps of the World. 2013, 6; ©werajoe/Shutterstock Images, 7; ©Casper1774 Studio/Shutterstock Images, 9; ©Dorling Kindersley/Thinkstock, 10; ©Joseph M. Arseneau/Shutterstock Images, 11; ©Aleksandar Todorovic/Shutterstock Images, 12; ©len4foto/CanStockPhoto, 15; ©Arun Roisri/Shutterstock Images, 16; ©Wang LiQiang/Shutterstock Images, 19; ©Pierre Jean Durieu/Dreamstime.com, 20; ©julianwphoto/CanStockPhoto, 21; ©Dave Montreuil/Shutterstock Images, 23; ©kajornyot/Shutterstock Images, 25; ©Nadezhda1906/Shutterstock Images, 27; ©Byelikova/CanStockPhoto, 2

Library of Congress Cataloging-in-Publication Data

Gray, Susan Heinrichs, author.
Hornbill / Susan H. Gray.
    pages cm. — (Exploring our rainforests)
  Summary: "Introduces facts about hornbills, including physical features, habitat, life cycle, food, and threats to these rainforest creatures. Photos, captions, and keywords supplement the narrative of this informational text."—Provided by publisher.
  Audience: Ages 8-12.
  Audience: Grades 4 to 6.
  ISBN 978-1-63188-975-2 (hardcover) — ISBN 978-1-63362-014-8 (pbk.) — ISBN 978-1-63362-053-7 (pdf) — ISBN 978-1-63362-092-6 (ebook) 1. Hornbills—Juvenile literature. I. Title.

  QL696.C729G73 2014
  598.7'8—dc23   2014020997

Cherry Lake Publishing would like to acknowledge the work of
The Partnership for 21st Century Skills. Please visit www.p21.org
for more information.

Printed in the United States of America
Corporate Graphics

ABOUT THE AUTHOR

Susan H. Gray has a master's degree in zoology. She has worked in research and has taught college-level science classes. Susan has also written more than 140 science and reference books, but especially likes to write about animals. She and her husband, Michael, live in Cabot, Arkansas.

TABLE OF CONTENTS

CHAPTER 1

WALLED IN

Tap tap tap tap. A mother hornbill is building a wall. She has moved into a large, dark cavity inside a tree trunk. Tap tap tap. With her oversized beak, she's packing soft, sticky materials around the cavity's entrance. Tap tap tap tap.

The hornbill keeps at it until she's almost completely walled in. She leaves only a small opening. For the next few months, she will remain inside. She won't be searching for tasty fruits. She won't be sitting in any other trees. This magnificent bird won't be flying at all.

The hornbill mother waits with her eggs.

Instead, she will lay her eggs and keep them warm. She will peer out of the opening and wait for her mate. Throughout the day, he will bring her bits of food. When the chicks hatch, he will bring enough food for all of them.

Hornbills live in the warmer parts of Africa and Asia. There are more than 50 **species**. Some hornbills live in grasslands, while others live in forests. Hornbills are found in parts of China, Nepal, Thailand, Vietnam, and other countries. Many of the best-known species live in India, the Philippines, and Indonesia.

RANGE MAP

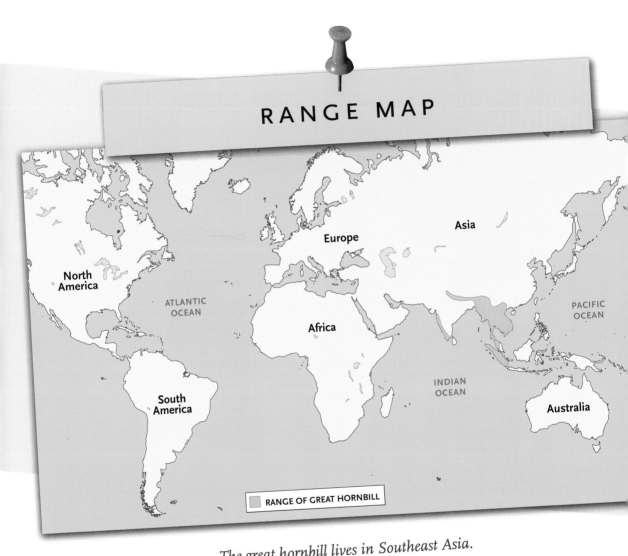

RANGE OF GREAT HORNBILL

North America

South America

ATLANTIC OCEAN

Europe

Africa

Asia

INDIAN OCEAN

PACIFIC OCEAN

Australia

The great hornbill lives in Southeast Asia.

Those that live in rainforests prefer to spend their time in the **canopy**. They pluck fruits from the upper branches of trees. They nest in tree cavities high above the ground.

This hornbill is tending to its chicks in the nest.

LOOK AGAIN

WHAT MIGHT BE AN ADVANTAGE TO BUILDING THE NEST INSIDE A TREE INSTEAD OF ON A BRANCH?

CHAPTER 2

WHAT A BEAK!

Hornbills are named for their remarkable beaks. The beak is large and curves downward. On top of the upper beak is a structure called the **casque**. This comes from a French word for "helmet." Different species have casques of different shapes and sizes. The white-crowned hornbill's casque is so small it is barely noticeable. The casque of the helmeted hornbill looks like a blocky mass atop the bill. And the rhinoceros hornbill has an impressive upward-curving casque.

The casque appears to be a heavy structure, but it

The rhinoceros hornbill has a huge casque.

isn't. In most birds, it contains a delicate bony network with lots of air spaces. Scientists are not sure why hornbills have these structures. Some believe they might help to increase the sound of the birds' songs and calls.

Hornbills are quite talented at using their beaks. They can tug both large and small fruits from branches. They are able to pick up insects and lizards, and snag flying squirrels. The beaks also serve as construction tools. The birds use them to plaster over the entrances to their nesting cavities.

BODY DIAGRAM

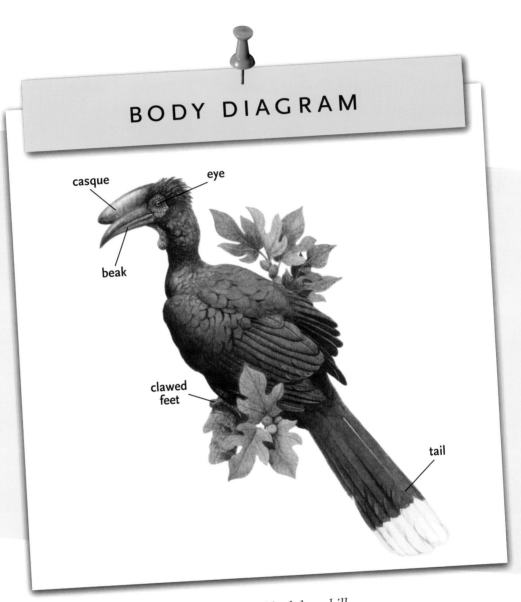

casque

eye

beak

clawed
feet

tail

This is a wattled black hornbill.

[21ST CENTURY SKILLS LIBRARY]

The hornbill has long feathers to protect its eyes.

Hornbills appear to have long eyelashes. These are not hairs, however. They are actually special feathers that are unusually thin. Still, they do the same job as human eyelashes. They protect the eyes from dust and dirt.

The birds' feathers contain only one **pigment**, a dark substance called melanin. Different amounts of melanin cause the feathers to be white, gray, brown, or black. But some species are quite colorful. For example, the great hornbill has bright yellow or orange patches on its feathers. The female wreathed hornbill's throat is blue, while the male's is yellow, and its eyes are encircled by red. Where do those colors come from?

Some hornbills have large blue throats.

The blue throats and red eye patches are nothing more than colorful bald spots. These areas are not feathered at all. Some birds have brightly colored skin patches. But yellow and orange feathers are a different story. The birds apply these colors themselves!

Hornbills (and most other birds) have oil glands at the base of their tails. Lying just beneath the skin, these glands release oil through small openings. Birds scrub their necks, faces, or beaks across the area and pick up the oil. Then they stroke the oil over their bodies, wings, and legs, which keeps their feathers in good shape. In hornbills, the oil is yellow or orange in color. Every time the birds **preen**, they are touching up their bright colors.

Hornbills come in all sizes. The smallest are the dwarf hornbills of Africa, which are smaller than crows. Among the largest is the great hornbill that lives in the rainforests of India. It has a wingspan of 5.8 feet (1.8 meters).

GO DEEPER

UNLIKE OTHER BIRDS, THE HORNBILL'S FIRST TWO NECK BONES ARE FUSED TOGETHER. HOW WOULD FUSED NECK BONES BENEFIT HORNBILLS?

CHAPTER 3

FILLING THE BILL

Hornbills devour many different foods. In the rainforests, they feed on insects, small birds, flying squirrels, fish, and reptiles. Their main food, though, is fruit. Hornbills get plenty of water, fat, and sugar from the fruits they choose.

Some hornbills appear to have their own favorite fruits. In the rainforests of India, hornbills fill up on figs. Great hornbills even choose their favorite fig trees. Then they scare off the wreathed hornbills that come to feed on that tree.

Hornbills catch lizards and eat them.

Hornbills eat fruit they find in the trees.

Scientists have studied these birds' diets. They have found that hornbills feed on almost 750 different species of plants. Many of these plants produce fruits loaded with seeds. The hornbills either spit them out or swallow them whole. The seeds pass through their digestive systems and end up in their droppings.

As it turns out, seed-swallowing birds are great for keeping the rainforests going. Hornbills traveling through the trees will drop seeds everywhere. In time, the seeds sprout, and new little fruit trees begin to grow.

Like most other birds, hornbills store food in an organ called the crop. From there, food can move to the next organ to be broken down. Or it might be **regurgitated**. A male hornbill stores food in his crop to bring back to the nest. There, he bobs his head up and down to help him regurgitate the food for the chicks.

THINK ABOUT IT
WHICH WOULD BE A MORE ENERGY-RICH FOOD FOR A HORNBILL—INSECTS OR FRUIT?

CHAPTER 4

THE HORNBILL'S LIFE

Long before they begin a family, male hornbills must find mates. During this time, males and females may call out to each other. They may also chase one another through the trees. Sometimes several males court the same female. So to win her over, a smart male must use his head. Either while perching or in flight, competing males will whack one another with their casques. Losing males fly off to find mates somewhere else. The victor wins a mate for life.

Soon after the pair forms, the birds search out a good

Hornbills pair up to raise their chicks.

nesting place, usually a hole in the side of a tree, high above the forest floor. A good hole cannot be too tight or too roomy. It must be big enough for the female and chicks to move comfortably. Once a good home is found, the female enters and the wall building begins.

The male and female work together on this task. They use a mix of mashed-up fruit, mud, and their own droppings for the "plaster." Beginning with the rim of the hole, they use their bills to tap the goo into place. This continues until only a small opening—often just a slit—remains.

Soon after she is walled in, the female lays her eggs. Large birds such as the rhinoceros hornbill lay only one or two. The smaller types of hornbills may lay four or five.

The hornbill nests are inside trees.

For the next few weeks, the female keeps her eggs warm. Meanwhile, her mate searches the forest for food. He brings fruit to her and feeds her through the slit in the wall. When the eggs hatch, the male steps up his activity. Back and forth he flies, bringing enough fruit for everyone. The brown hornbill of India uses a slightly different system. The male has helpers. His male offspring from earlier years also bring food to their mom and younger **siblings**.

Over time, the nest gets a little crowded. Such a place would tend

This hornbill is dropping food into the nest.

to get filthy as well. But the hornbill knows how to keep her place clean. She twists around inside the cavity to release her droppings through the slit. She picks up the droppings of her young and tosses them out, too.

Eventually, it's time for someone to leave the nest. Great hornbill mothers break out, leaving their young to re-seal the wall. The mother then helps her mate carry food back to the nest. At about 4 months of age, it's time for the young to leave. The Malabar gray hornbill operates a little differently. Everyone breaks out together after 3 months.

At first, the young birds are poor fliers. After all, they've never left the nest before. Their parents stay close by, guarding and feeding them until they are strong. Over time, the young birds become expert fliers. They also learn where to find the best fruit trees. For some species, growing up is a slow process. It may take several years before they are adults, ready to find mates.

Once pairs do form, the birds remain together for life. Throughout their lives, they "flirt" with each other. They call back and forth, perch together, and rub their bills against each other. This flirting builds loyalty and trust. These traits matter a lot, especially during the times when the female depends entirely on her mate for food.

This is a young western red-billed hornbill.

LOOK AGAIN

HERE IS A YOUNG HORNBILL. DO YOU THINK IT WOULD MAKE A GOOD PET? WHY OR WHY NOT?

CHAPTER 5

WHAT THE FUTURE HOLDS

The future is uncertain for most hornbill species. A very young bird may become a meal for an eagle or other rainforest **predator**. But this is not the chief danger these birds face. The two main threats are hunting and **habitat** loss.

People who live in the rainforests often hunt hornbills for meat. They also collect their feathers or bills to use in ceremonies. **Poachers** might kill the birds simply to get their beaks and casques. They sell these body parts for high prices. Poachers might also collect live birds to sell as pets.

Hornbills have bright feathers that people sometimes collect illegally.

Habitat destruction is an even greater problem. Hornbills of the rainforest cannot live anywhere else. They depend on the rainforest for fruit, safety, and good nesting holes. But in many places, loggers are cutting down their trees. Sometimes they only cut trees from the edges of the forest, but other times loggers cut down huge sections of trees.

Farming is another problem. People clear rainforest land to plant crops. As a result, many trees come down. Some of them had good nesting holes. Hornbills use the

The great hornbill's biggest threat is humans.

same nesting holes year after year. So the birds are left with fewer and fewer places to lay eggs and raise their young.

Fortunately, some people are working to protect these birds. Scientists at the Malaysian Nature Society are working to understand hornbills' needs. Volunteers are also educating the public about the importance of saving them.

In Thailand, Dr. Pilai Poonswad has convinced native people to stop killing the birds. She has taught

At this aviary in Indonesia, families can interact with hornbills who live there.

them how to gather data on hornbills and how to protect the birds' nests. One of her best helpers used to be a poacher. Now he teaches people about the importance of hornbills.

In a way, even the hornbills are looking out for the rainforest. Scientists have noticed that when hornbills fly far away from home, looking for food, they spread new seeds there. The further they spread the seeds, the more they may be helping the rainforest to recover.

Much remains to be done to protect these birds. Many hornbill populations appear to be shrinking. But now, people who live in the rainforest are protecting the birds. Perhaps this idea will spread. Hornbills have been here for many years. We hope they will be here for many more.

Hornbills depend on trees for survival.

LOOK AGAIN

LOOK CLOSELY AT THIS PHOTOGRAPH OF HORNBILLS LIVING IN THEIR NATURAL HABITAT. DO YOU SEE NATURAL RESOURCES THAT SHOULD BE PROTECTED FROM HUMANS?

THINK ABOUT IT

- While stuck in the nest cavity, some females molt. That means they shed their feathers and grow new ones. Why would this be an especially good time to molt?

- Some scientists say that hornbills live to be 30 years old. Others claim they reach 40 or even 50 years of age. Why is it so hard for scientists to figure out how old the birds get?

- Chapter 4 covers the hornbill's nest. With such a closed-in nest, eggs will not roll out. What might be some other safety features of this nest?

- If poachers catch or kill a male hornbill, could this cause other hornbills to die? Explain your answer.

- Loggers cut down rainforest trees because they can sell the wood. What are some ways to stop people from buying rainforest wood?

LEARN MORE

FURTHER READING

Johnson, Jinny. *1000 Things You Should Know about Birds*. Essex, UK: Miles Kelly Publishing, 2008.

Salmansohn, Pete, and Stephen W. Kress. *Saving Birds: Heroes Around the World*. Gardiner, ME: Tilbury House Publishers, 2003.

Sen, Moen. *Designed to Survive: All About Beaks*. New Delhi, India: The Energy and Resources Institute, 2011.

WEB SITES

Audubon Animals: Great Hornbill
www.auduboninstitute.org/animals/asian-domain/great-hornbill-1957
Look at this site for information and fun facts about the great hornbill.

Rhinoceros Hornbill
http://kids.mongabay.com/animal-profiles/rhinoceros_hornbill.html
Check out this site for information on the rhinoceros hornbill, its life, and its nesting habits.

San Diego Zoo Animals: Hornbill
http://animals.sandiegozoo.org/animals/hornbill
Look here for some amazing photos of hornbills, and some cool facts about their lives.

GLOSSARY

canopy (KAN-uh-pee) the cover formed by the leafy upper branches in a forest

casque (KASK) a helmetlike structure on the head of some animals

habitat (HAB-i-tat) the place where a plant or animal naturally lives

pigment (PIG-muhnt) a substance used to color something

poachers (POH-cherz) people who kill wild animals illegally

predator (PRED-uh-tur) an animal that hunts and eats other animals

preen (PREEN) to groom feathers by using the bill

regurgitated (rih-GUR-ji-tate-ed) to have brought food that has been swallowed back up to the mouth

siblings (SIB-lingz) brothers and sisters

species (SPEE-seez) a particular type, or kind, of plant or animal

INDEX